WHAT THE TRAPEZE ARTIST TRUSTS

WHAT THE TRAPEZE ARTIST TRUSTS

Poems by

MALAIKA KING ALBRECHT

Press 53
Winston-Salem

Press 53, LLC
PO Box 30314
Winston-Salem, NC 27130

First Edition

Copyright © 2012 by Malaika King Albrecht

A Tom Lombardo Poetry Selection

All rights reserved, including the right of reproduction in whole or in part in any form. For permission, contact author at editor@Press53.com, or at the address above.

Cover design by Kevin Morgan Watson

Cover art, "Trapeze Artists in Circus"
lithograph by Calvert Litho. Co., 1890. Public Domain.

Author photo by Amani Albrecht

Printed on acid-free paper

ISBN 978-1-935708-54-4

To my daughters Amani and Serena.

Acknowledgments

The author wishes to thank the following editors, journals, websites, and books where these poems or versions of these poems first appeared:

Arsenic Lobster: "To the Man with His Back to the Chapel"
Asheville Poetry Review: "Sound Knows its Place in the Air" and "On the Shore at Holden Beach"
Bay Leaves: "How to Walk Right Through a Woman," first place winner of 2010 James Larkin Pearson Contest for Free Verse
Best Poem: A Poetry Journal: "On Your Birth Day"
Dead Mule: "Leaving the Island," "Troublesome Creek," The Earth Is My New Pair of Shoes," and "Loving the Dark Cloud"
Empowerment4Women: "The Present Moment," "The Road Is Home," and "A Moment's Awareness"
International Poetry Review: "A Box Made in Autumn"
Kakalak: An Anthology of Carolina Poets: "Swift Water"
Kritya: "Late Night News"
Literary Mama: "Sweat Test for Cystic Fibrosis"
Piedmont Literary Review: "Genealogy"
Pirene's Fountain: "Beyond the Clover Meadow" Pushcart Prize nominee, and "The Secret Keeper"
Platte Valley Review: "The Frozen Dialect of the Tundra"
Poetry Southeast: "The Magician's Assistant," first place winner
Poetry Warrior: "Dear Stranger, This Is My Intimate"
Press 53 Open Awards Anthology: "Sweat Test for Cystic Fibrosis," "Swift Water," and "On Your Birth Day," second place winner
Press 53 Spotlight Anthology: "The Drowned Husband" and "About That First Step"
Prime Number Magazine: "My Daughter's Keepsake Rock"
Quarterly West: "Tenses"
Soundings Review: "It Wasn't Easy to be Hit," "Tying Rocks to Clouds," and "The Between Places"
The Pedestal Magazine: "The Dusting"

What the Trapeze Artist Trusts

Introduction by Tom Lombardo, Poetry Series Editor   xi

I. The Secret Keeper

Dear Stranger, This Is My Intimate	3
Castaways	4
You Have Spoken of Water	5
Sound Knows Its Place in the Air	6
The Secret Keeper	7
Deep Water Horizon	8
What Hurts Must Be Transformed	9
On Your Birth Day	10
Sweat Test for Cystic Fibrosis	11
My Recurring Pool Dream	12
About That First Step	13
On the Shore at Holden Beach	14
Standing on the Coupeville Pier	16

II. Keeping Silence

To the Pitcher	19
The Frozen Dialect of the Tundra	20
Loving the Dark Cloud	21
The Magician's Assistant	22
Tenses	23
Come and Tell Me Why You're Leaving Me	25
How To Walk Right Through a Woman	26
Swift Water	27
The Drowned Husband	28
Leaving the Island	30
The Consequences of Silence	31
Beautiful, Beautiful! Magnificent Desolation	32

III. The Present

Genealogy	35
What Grief and a Fever Bring	36
Troublesome Creek	37
The Present Moment	38
It Wasn't Easy To Be Hit	39
How I Came to Me	40
Late Night News	41
Basic Math	42
Training the Mind in Lotus Position	43
When I Left My Country,	44
The Road Is Home	45
The Earth Is My New Pair of Shoes	46
The Keeper of the Well	47

IV. The Broken and the Lost

Baptism	53
The Broken and the Lost	54
That September Day	55
What We're Made Of	56
Beyond the Clover Meadow	58
Of Lost Sheep, Lost Coins and Lost Sons	59
Rocks to Clouds	60
A Box Made in Autumn	61
The Dusting	62
To the Man With His Back to the Chapel	63
The Sunken Narrative	64
My Daughter's Keepsake Rock	65

Introduction
Tom Lombardo, Poetry Series Editor

One of the rewards of my job at Press 53 is to discover new poets working in obscurity. When I find one as good as Malaika King Albrecht, I feel like I've jumped the moon. It is my great pleasure to introduce the poetry world to Ms. Albrecht's breakout collection.

Malaika King Albrecht dreams of larger worlds. Worlds where the sea rushes into "the silence between words…that space between what / happened and what we believe." Worlds where there are "53 words for lost / but only one for found." Worlds where "no one catches the name / of where we go, where we began."

At the outset, Ms. Albrecht lets her dress slip from her shoulders and whispers so we must lean close to hear about worlds full of her sins and her prayers, her cravings, the bitter bite of sea salt on her tongue, the stings of insects and people, and her propensity for filling her living room with the dead. Her worlds become studies of losses in slow motion, as when she describes being the invisible woman whose crumbling marriage slides through her hands like sand, the man walking right through her as if she were immaterial air. That world is a shipwreck and she is buried at sea.

The waves and tides sweep the shore clean while footprints on the moon will last forever. Somewhere between those two extremes, she bounces between the tight fist of a Braxton Hicks or the tight fist of a departing lover.

That same ocean that sweeps clean the past may also redeem the past:

The ocean wind blows you away.
Let go. Free yourself like the braided
strings that no longer hold kites.

Introduction by Tom Lombardo

In her Holy Equation of Everything, "the universe returns/ all to earth."

At edge of that world, what does a trapeze artist trust?

Reading this collection, dear reader, you will learn that Ms. Albrecht, like a magician's assistant, finds her escape from the direst outcomes, noticing that redemption happens

as surely
as endless circles ripple
from a dropped stone.

She casts a net of words that the trapeze artist hopes—while in midair—is no longer needed so that she might say, "I am in possession of myself."

This debut collection will cleanse your world with its ripples and waves, and, like the footprints on the moon, will leave an ineradicable imprint on your universe.

I.

The Secret Keeper

Dear Stranger, This Is My Intimate

letter to you that will not change
you or even a fly's flight shadow
across this page. We have awakened
mid-dream to find each other here.
You say, "Write me somewhere."

This is where I let my dress
slip from my shoulders and whisper
so you must lean close to me to hear
and then even closer until I'm only moist
warm air along your neck and into your ear.

Castaways

I dream of a fire burning with no smoke,
and though I know many words have sin
in them, I still find them pleasing to say.

Do you know how it feels when you touch me?
The map you create of my body
charts my feet as rivers, my knees
as lakes and my arms as ocean.

I'll swim to the raft when I must,
and tell no one of our island,
of the ocean waves within,
of the sand that spills from my shoes
and scatters like prayers as I walk away.

You Have Spoken of Water

The way rain sounds hitting Highway 50
in an August thunderstorm. The way

Willow Creek just before it freezes
smells like winter mint. The way water

tastes after falling down Copper Mountain
and into your hands. The way it feels

to step into a hot spring in winter. The way
Menokin Bay can hold the image of the whole

sky and a single eagle. You have shown me
water, and yet, I thirst.

Sound Knows Its Place in the Air

You don't have a soul. You are a soul. You have a body.
— C.S. Lewis

I.

Seeing becomes a study
of loss in slow motion.
A single grain of sand falls
and another and another.
I'm less myself today,
but don't take it personally.
A handful of sand—
not a beach and yet
all I can hold.

II.

There are no longer angels
in the flames. We left
the fires untended on the beach,
some have gone out.
I cannot invent
the exact light
of Your name.

III.

We are inconsequential
to the dance, but music
fills the air around us,
ocean waves, heart beats.
Grace lifts itself from the hems
of our tongues.
We listen with
our whole bodies.
I will not say Your name
though I believe
it was You who called me.

The Secret Keeper

> *think how long I have known these*
> *deep dead leaves*
> *without meeting you.*
> — W.S. Merwin

She will cradle your handful of bees,
the fire ants, your lemon slices,
and the pale green luna moth.

She will hold your mouthful of marbles,
spent matches and kindling,
the sorrow jar, and a single key.

She will carry your field of dandelions,
the slice of borrowed sky, and your twisted
river in hers until you meet again.

Deep Water Horizon

this is the recurring
        where the animal
meets the human
        a dolphin
in the shape
        of a woman swimming
the sea in her hands

        her hands are turtles
her hair, a net
        where she catches herself
thinking of the slick
        and sticky dark

this is the recurring
        she is flying
the wind in her hands
        her hands are pelicans

that dive and cannot
        rise again
sink like sleep
        the mud says
i will kiss your eyelids

What Hurts Must Be Transformed

A spell on every tongue, the hidden
pink taste of secrets. My lips
like sea shells shut tight.
Alone, I sing in my sleep and wake
to the whale in my belly
sounding the deep song of longing,
the bite of sea salt on my tongue.
Oh mouth, temple of hunger, of thirst,
of prayer, sing to the pearl
that becomes the iridescent flash
of a sunfish leaping from my throat.

On Your Birth Day

I ride the steady refrain
of your heart beat, its simple
dance on the screen, a comfort
when contractions begin.
The song changes to a rap, a
beat, a pause, a
beat
and silence. The room
becomes a beehive
of nurses, doctors, equipment.
                        A mask
on my face, I'm adrift, bobbing
on a huge bed in a sea
of activity. *Push*. I can't
remember what the word
means. I think *push, gush
rush*—the sounds of water.
I hear a gurgle
and then a wet cry. This is how
it feels to spill the whole of you—
an ocean wave—
that knocks me back to shore.

Sweat Test for Cystic Fibrosis

What to call this battery box, wires dangling
electrodes? A polygraph. A torture device.
The usual white linoleum in this small room
hot as a summer attic and on a metal table,
the box that my eldest daughter names *Pirate*,
saying it looks like a face with an eye patch.

The nurse doesn't name it. She explains,
*The sweat sample's collected by using liquid
on a patch of skin.* She touches my daughter's
forearm. *Painless. Tingles with a weak electrical
current.* She attaches the electrodes.

My younger daughter, spins around
and around, chanting, *Dizzy. Dizzy.*
The machine hums like an electric razor.
I brush Amani's hair from her damp forehead.
stroking her hair, my fingers do their usual work,
finding tangles and gently working strands free.

How rarely I notice myself breathing or
holding my breath. Last night I was thinking
about the soul, its papery home.
Walking in the house I know so well
I can navigate in the dark, I thought:
All that I love most moves nearby.
One child snoring. The other quiet as a pillow.
I freeze in her doorway. Wait. Then see
her chest rise, a small wave.

My Recurring Pool Dream

As my child
holds her arms
high above

her head, she says,
Catch me, mom,
and I

patiently
stand waist deep
arms wide,

wait for the moment
she leaps and

About That First Step

At the cliff's edge, the dancer
wonders what the trapeze artist
trusts between bars.
Maybe she hopes, midair,
there's no longer need.

On the Shore at Holden Beach

I.

High tide reveals
in every beginning,
an end.

The sea asks, *How strong
will you stand?* Rises and falls
all around you.

No matter where
we die, we're buried
at sea.

Once my daughter nearly drowned
blue lips and
the sound of waves
inside her chest.
             Cut adrift,
we clung to a hospital bed
for three days until she
thrashed ashore-
said *I want to go home.*

II.

She finds a whole
sand dollar in the surf,
places it in my palm. *Don't
lose it, mommy. Squeeze tight.*

I say *No, it will break.*

How to teach her
that a fist
is how life catches us
in the jar of our own desire
to hold, to count
what we think is ours.
I show her, *Hold your hands
with the sand dollar
between your palms.*

Like we're praying, she says
walking gently back to shore.

Standing on the Coupeville Pier

The green fishing line
strung post to post
along the wooden pier
sings, strummed to a low
hum by Puget Sound's wind.
Nothing remains still.
Mirrored clouds unravel
like the mind over time,
and water stitches
and unstiches itself
along the rocky shore.
Small changes happen as surely
as endless circles ripple
from a dropped stone.
Imperceptible as loss
but gone nonetheless.

II.

Keeping Silence

To the Pitcher

You are part of this dream—
not the running in quicksand
or the small animals we've forgotten
to feed in a closet—but our
sycamore tree in flames in the front yard.

My ribcage, a baseball glove,
I've run home a few times
to check the stove, fireplace, grill.
Where's the fire? you ask
as I stand there burning.

The Frozen Dialect of the Tundra

How wet when melted and yet now
it cannot quench. What it does not

swallow like rocks, crops, or whole
villages, it shuts out in the cold.

Damn we say and we mean *God*.
Mercy we write, white on white

broken letters in the snow
glinting like petroglyphs.

We say *Ice* which means do not yield.
In northern nowhere, the flint sky

has no spark for us, and what we love
most doesn't have wings. The ground

knows why we hold each other
shivering and only the wind is never full.

Loving the Dark Cloud

Though I want the meadowlark
singing in the field of winter
wheat tangled as my hair in wind,
I love a dark cloud, its grey foreboding
under my left shoulder blade.
The way thunder trembles my ribs
and rumbles down my legs.
The way tension and the promise
of release string my spine.

Loving the dark cloud is like loving
a rock. How it will only speak
its persistent silence to the river bank.
How it resists touch but holds
your warmth for a moment. Loving the dark
cloud is like loving the minnows in your hands,
the broken emerald in your throat,
or the blue moon butterflies haloing your head.
The dark cloud's torrent sweeps me away
into everything I am not.

The Magician's Assistant

I am scarf after scarf
in his nothing-up-my-sleeves trick.
I am behind-the-ears quarter,
rabbit in his hat
and wand that never fails.

I am his black box
disappearing and reappearing
who enters me. I am handcuffs
and blindfold that he escapes.

I am the chosen card
memorized and ripped apart,
suddenly whole again in his hands.
I am levitating, doves flying
from my rib cage
that he sawed so cleanly.

I am the hush that precedes
the good trick, then applause. I am
his cut cord, restored.
I am the final word—
his abracadabra of finales.

TENSES

Walking along the canal wall,
he and I don't hold hands.
Currents catch the sunset,
drag light toward ocean.

The limbs of trees swim
the surface. Mullets jump
branches, and sheepsheads
thrash barnacles

to split them open. We sit.
He slips his hand into a velvet bag
and places one cold stone
between us, a Viking rune.

Who needs stone to say loss?
I know that night, one day
stronger, will fall on us.
I know I'm more lonely

than I've ever been alone.
Tonight, at a party, he'll drink
vodka and toss more runes
to reveal another's future.

I know the other woman's body
will fill our bedroom, press
against my chest until I can
no longer breathe next to him.

Chasing glass lizards, earlier,
he caught only a tail that danced,
bodiless, in his hand.
When it stilled, he dropped it.

I say I've learned to read him;
what no longer moves for him,
doesn't move him.
Because he's heard, he's quiet.

A crane lands across the canal,
ripples water whose concentric
circles will taste this wall.
The present's been unwanted

as any truth. He says,
Why predict the inevitable?
As he stands, I throw the stone
across water, and twice, it skips.

Come and Tell Me Why You're Leaving Me

This is how to fill the living room
with dead people: a spinning
disk, unraveling years like a snag.
What will I sing? he asks.

Now the only thing a gambler needs
Is a suitcase and trunk
And the only time he's satisfied

Voices spill and eat the air cold,
the piano, a familiar hand on a shoulder.
In this dream, we sing again
with a younger brother's drunken song.

Well, I got one foot
on the platform,
the other foot on the train.

How To Walk Right Through a Woman

I can't remember the curse that made me
invisible. I only know that one day
he held my hand, and then another,

my hand slipped through his like sand.
I stayed in the room, an empty vase
in the dark and not even moonlight could find me.

He may have sensed my presence
as he stepped around me and around me
packing his books, clothes, toothbrush.

By morning he could walk right through
as if I were an open window,
a door, the immaterial air.

Swift Water

The boundaries between land
and water loosen; the earth cannot
absorb more. In a canoe,

a neighbor paddles by, waves
without smiling. Over flooded yards
and streets, chimney swifts,

black boomerangs, cut through air.
The swifts careen from our chimney,
which they've filled with nests,

staccato notes, and beating wings.
No one sent this flood. Walking
toward me, my husband created a wake

in the living room. No one sought
to teach a lesson. I learn anyway.
I say swifts eat and drink on the wing,

snap twigs midair without pause
to build their nests. We will rip up carpet,
throw away the contents of bottom shelves:

letters from the separation, photographs
unnoticed for years, our wedding book.
Soon the swifts will whirl in a circle

above the house, funnel down at dusk
for the night. Clocks stopped, we stand on the deck,
the familiar warmth of arms lightly touching
in the gray remnants of a just passed storm.

The Drowned Husband

With him I feel like a gray
dress with long sleeves.
My hands stack salt grains
on the table while we eat.

One evening when the ocean
splashes over the dunes,
he doesn't wade back
across the flooded yard
home again from the sea.

The wind bangs all night
like someone knocking on wood
until it rips the screen door
from its hinges.

A month later, I think
I see him as a sea bass,
wishless, lit and unlit
by the sun through waves.

When our daughters come home,
I point to a jar full of water, say,
Here is your father.

One morning the jar falls and shatters.
Water spills everywhere.
Then I know he's free.

He's all water now.
The sheets smell of him,
and if I wash them, it's only worse.

I stop washing the laundry.
I stop washing the dishes.
I stop washing my hands.

He's everywhere. This damn rain,
and when the rain stops,
the humid air, so full of it, so full of himself.

Leaving the Island

On the tree stump beside his bed, a jar of sharks
waits for something to break. This is how it is
when you're shipwrecked. One night he calls me
into longing, into flesh. *Woman, it's an act of love,
this standing rose in a hand.* For a while, paradise,
but the rose becomes a conch, and the hand, a swordfish.

I see ships in every cloud. Each hour becomes the thirst
hour on the beach, and us, without cupped hands or sails.
This is how to swim, he says one day and holds me
under a wave. On the shore, he sets fire to every limb
of driftwood. The rocks write my name
on the beach, and I sink, my pockets full.

The Consequences of Silence

the spaces between the wooden fence rungs
the sunlight slicing a path through knotted clouds
the sky shards blue amid reddening leaves
the dry spots of dirt between rain drops
the distance between bodies on a walk
between my right hand and your left
the sound between words
the distance between letters
who will remember the truth
that space between what
happened and what we believe
these words took moments to read
that's how it ends

Beautiful, Beautiful! Magnificent Desolation

—Buzz Aldrin

Stare at the sky, that darkest of blacks
above a terrain that casts shades of gray,
a touch of brown, and utter emptiness
where even the rocks hide their shadows.
A landscape where no leaf has drifted,
no caterpillar rippled grass,
the silence of vacuum dynamite's
no louder than a falling snowflake.
Under the crescent of an earthrise,
a man returns to his space ship
with the moon in his pockets,
leaving footprints that will last
longer than his life.

III.

The Present

Genealogy

Before my mother arrived in Tanzania,
my father mailed a tsetse fly,
wrote, *It's warm, and I sleep well.*

Playing guitar, my parents sang
my name, a Swahili song, together
in a treefort suite above rhinos.

My mother's mother and her mother
sent a dark blood to flame my veins,
prayed I'd be woman-strong.

My mother's father cleaned his rig,
said spit and sweat make a day.
I heard his words in her.

My father's mother combed her hair;
its signal redness caught the wind.
I grabbed the hair and rubbed my head.

My father's father built a mobile,
planets and a sun that turned
above my head. In shimmering night,
I dreamed of larger worlds.

What Grief and a Fever Bring

In the shimmering I find a thin place
where we almost touch in the February sleet,
where a cardinal lands, a splash of red on snow,
where the air for a moment's as warm
as my forehead, where I hear
a bit of song caught in my hair.
What else is left to do but accept
the unacceptable, to lean into
that wet wind as unknown horses
canter toward us? They know
the beauty of impermanence.
I promise to recognize you
in a stranger's laughter.
After a handful of Irish dirt
and a final duet, we depart. Wings
burst from my shoulder blades.

Troublesome Creek

The marsh tide calls me,
and cat tails rattle in the wind
when I turn restless in our bed.

I've kept all the bird calls I've ever heard
in the cup of my ear
to spill into your empty
hands as you sleep.

More important than the birds' names,
each song has a shape—
blue triangles of eagles,
the gray loops of doves.

Maybe you'll dream of how shapes
build a house or how colors
find each other in the painting of us
on the pier earlier today.

I follow the fog past the tulip poplar tree
dropping white flowers into the water.
Even at night, I find the crossing bridge
where the water stops to listen
to its own falling.

When I'm lost in the waves
that sift the silt along the banks,
I find myself in the red twist
of a whippoorwill's call cutting air.

The Present Moment

My mind is a jar
of muddy water.

Please understand
my lack of clarity.

I am not the sky
holding the universe.

I am not the ocean
holding the sky. I am

doing nothing, and it's not
easy to do. See the water

in my cupped hands
emptying itself of me.

It Wasn't Easy To Be Hit

by lightning. Storms strike quickly
like tempers in our family of redheads.

When this squall rolled over the butte,
a dark fist closing on our small town,

I danced down Main Street in my aluminum foil
dress and matching hat, swinging a yellow umbrella.

Friday the 13th and my 13th birthday,
I knew it was my lucky day. A flash,

and I was jigging. I thought, *Baby,
I'm on fire. I'm a live wire.*

I fell to my knees and floated above
myself light as smoke before waking

in the hospital. You could say I'm lucky
now. I can draw lightning out of

the clear blue sky. My hands
are sparklers, and electric sockets

snake to touch my fingertips
with hot tongues. I spark God,

flame-headed and wild
always dancing in a light rain.

How I Came to Me

No longer am I
dispossessed
or repossessed.

I am possessed.
I am in possession
of myself.

I am self-possessed.
The sun rises in my throat
and burns a perfect hole

in my forehead
where cliff swallows roost.
Each rain drop falls

perfectly into place
on the greenness of me.
I want you to know

that at this edge
of my life:
I will jump.

I will jump.
I will jump
and I will fly.

Late Night News

We're sleeping. You don't wake up.
Someone is calling my name. Am I awake?
Someone is calling me
names. We have too many names
and some we won't answer to. We
have much to answer for.

The world is asleep. How else
to explain what is happening? The world
sleeps loudly. Like a baby. Someone else's baby
on the page, the TV screen, the ground.

There are many children. The long hallway, darker
than night, is growing longer, is growing more doors
which means more choices, which means I stand
in front of the many doors. Which door,
which child?

This place loses mothers, fathers, brothers, sisters,
sons and daughters. I don't know where the bodies
come from or are going, spilling from beds,
from buildings, from every earthly opening.

Our footprints are everywhere, even the moon
and the sea's floor. We have touched the world,
and we are bored. We're in your home now,
reading your email and taking lint samples
from your socks, unfolding and folding your underwear.

The last hiding place of snow will not be here
for long. The polar bears are diving and diving and diving.
Where can we walk in this watery place? Each hurt person
is a stone in our pockets. We are all wounded, trying
to stay awake, treading water. Sing loudly, and
in between songs, hold the dying.

Basic Math

The currency of the universe
      is limitless probability.
X happens. Whatever x equals:
      a Bodhi tree,
White Shell Mountain, the Dead Sea
      or my life.

A single cell divides. A creature
      slides from sea to soil
multiplies, diversifies. In the beginning,
      there was the word,
and that word was and always
      will be *Yes*.

Yes to weather patterns and ocean currents.
      Yes to amethyst
crystals, intracloud lightning, the Ganges river.
      Yes to the systems
of blood vessels branching our bodies
      like tree limbs.
Yes to fractals and the infinite repetition—
      snowflake, ocean wave, honeycomb—
this intersection of beauty and function.

Holy Equation of Everything,
      I am grateful
for your additions, your subtractions.
      Here I am now.
      Here I am not.

Training the Mind in Lotus Position

My puppy chews on anything. I put
the puppy down and say, *Stay*.
She jumps up and runs in circles. I sit
the puppy back down. *Stay*.
My puppy races away.
Sometimes my puppy leaps up
and pees in the corner.
Sit. Stay. I start over again.

When I Left My Country,

there were 53 words for lost
and only 1 for found.
I built a city of post cards
and spent stamps. I hid
the word *home* under my tongue
and slept in no one's room.
I split the miles between us,
searching for middle ground.

The desert teaches me to want
so little and yet I want it even more.
In the shimmer, hope plays tricks,
leaves me rubbing sand in my eyes.
Maybe I see you. Maybe I don't.
I draw a map of what together
looks like with its plain white door.
I knock.

The Road Is Home

To start a journey we begin
with this moment, a Now
that has just left and is no longer
with this word. Are we on the same page?

I know where I am, he once said
because I'm always, 'You are Here.'
See the red X on any map.
Wherever I go, there I am.
How can anyone ever be lost?

Sometimes along the way, the self
becomes a necklace
I've forgotten is strung around my neck
or sunglasses I've absently
pushed to the top of my head,
and am now asking,
Where are my sunglasses?

Neither shore's visible in the middle
of a long bridge. No one's getting
any younger. The traffic rolls
in one direction though sometimes I'm alone,
and I've forgotten in which direction I'm headed.
I've forgotten the traveler visiting this body.
I've forgotten about the ragged coat
I borrowed from someone so long ago.

I want to be the same person
who just left through this door years ago
but I'm changing even as I promise,
Nothing's different. If I return, I
won't be coming back as me.

The Earth Is My New Pair of Shoes

to Ansel Adams

A stone wind burnished the sky
and long clouds feathered
the blue expanse. The silver light
turned each blade of grass
and every particle of sand
a luminous metallic splendor.

There was nothing, however small,
that did not flash in the wind
that did not send arrows of light
through the glassy air. I was arrested
along the crunching path up the ridge
by an awareness of the light
caught on my skin and in my hair.

That moment I saw the detail
of the grasses, the small flotsam
of the forest, and the curves of the high
clouds streaming above the peaks.
I could say nothing in response,
but fit perfectly where I stood,
my feet in the dear dusty earth.

The Keeper of the Well

1. Fish

No one catches the name
of where we go, where we began.
Minnows slip from our hands
and the shimmering begins.

2. Cup

Every tree, every mountain, a ladder.
Sky, You are everywhere.
I'm on my knees. My empty hands
cupped full of You.

3. Bowl

Every cloud, a mirror
in the sky's endless bowl.
Come absence. I see your holes
shaped like me.

4. Lamb

Every seed, every drop
of rain. Each blade
of grass with its Angel
whispering, *Grow.*
I hear them soft as wool.

5. Lion

Every pebble, the reminder
of the remainder of kingdoms.
I feel the roar of sand
through an hourglass.

6. Well

I cast a net of words
into the endless pool
where I've watched
myself ripple.

7. Dirt

Know that the universe returns
all to earth. Dirt embraces
everyone no matter
what you've done
in this body.

8. Olive Branch

In every shell, the Voice
with lessons of water
of what it means to have
too little or too much.

9. Wine

What grows is always what
was planted. Twists of tendrils
climb an oak, and clusters of grapes
spill over. To fill the cup,
stomp.

10. Stained Glass

I stand, sit, kneel.
Color splashes
my body, frankincense,
my hair.

11. Knees

Here I most love You,
where you find me
ready for sleep,
my body a boat,
the lantern within
shining in the river of night.
I am not yet home.

12. Mustard Seed

Behold, not a single
seed in my hand.
Death's the guest
in each house
before me.

13. Desert

At the edge
the keeper waits
with a dipper
of cool water.

IV.

The Broken and the Lost

Baptism

A christening of broken glass
and bent metal—
the new Ford along an icy guardrail
on your first birthday. Your cries
from your car seat hive me
into the now, into the white
snap of my wrist bone, the taste
of lemons in the back of my throat,
and the air bag pinning me
into the driver's seat. A cascade
of sirens and someone opens
the passenger door, shouts,
Are you okay?
In the ambulance I think
it would have been enough
to skid along the ice, perhaps even
spin 360 degrees and stop
unharmed where we'd begun
with only the seat belt's bite
across my chest to remind me
of what ifs, to bring me to my knees
with less insistence than this
knowing how even a single scar
on you will be one on me.

The Broken and the Lost

I have woven a parachute out of everything broken
—William Stafford

I have jumped out
of the plane of my life,
falling like quartz
to break free
or break apart
along fracture lines
and build a beach
of what remains.
It's the lost things
I can't find
another use for:
his mother's jagged ring,
a 40th birthday card,
the heart-shaped stone.
What can be done
but to make a ghost
of what leaves
when the fog erases
the difference between
road and river
and drives us straight
into a swift swim?

That September Day

Even if all hawks vanish, their image
sleeps in the birds' souls. What sleeps
in us, the imprint of fear
deep as fight or flight?
Are you afraid? my sister asks.

I don't answer because she's safe
and didn't go to work today.
At the morning swim class,
my daughter leaps in like any other day.
Eight months pregnant, I roll into the water.

The water aerobics class sings
God Bless America, and I can't
remember the words. My daughter
practices the dead man's float
then dog paddles wildly towards an edge.

At home, she draws two standing rectangles
with ovals lodged in them. *Planes*, she says.
I feel the tight fist of Braxton Hicks.
The world spins beneath us, a dizzying
drop.

What We're Made Of

I. Dust

Creation, a scattering of mustard
seeds. By Whose hand, this life?
Death present as a sparrow in fog:
root   wing   root
wing

II. Apple

Know that the lovely scarlet ribbon
tangled in the tree's limbs
will unravel in a storm and snake
around your wrists. Eat
the garden.

III. Fig Leaf

Dark rag clouds knot
above the tree line,
and the west wind, a whip,
gives advice to a fire:
burn.

IV. Thorn

3 nails, a wound, a rib:
the answer strung along wood;
a delicate instrument, the body
sings of water—
of blood.

V. Bread

He is the image of forever
just beneath desire
in this river of hunger.
A rock, the son
rising,

dawn endless in its promises
of one last chance:
a present with a future, perfect
even after this
past.

Beyond the Clover Meadow

The gray horse from the other forest
knows that a storm can steal
breath from a sleeping mouth.
She leans into the bark of the dogwood,
her back against the wet wind. Awake.
If you want to live,
learn how to lean into the forest,
bury your face into the fallen
leaves until you are the color
of loss, until you can only
be seen close up
as the reflection on a beetle's shiny back.
In the forest the angels carry
ladders of light from cloud to cloud.
One day they will lower one
through the canopy of trees
break the gray between squalls
and you will climb. You will climb.

OF LOST SHEEP, LOST COINS AND LOST SONS

I've found water by the tug
of a willow branch,
gazed at moon-water
in a crystal bowl
long enough to lose myself
and find myself again.
Lessons in lost
number the same
as lessons in found.

I've seen the signs:
tossed chicken bones and runes,
read tea leaves and Tarot cards,
even the scatter of black birds in snow
is the gods writing to us.

You will be born.
You will go astray.
Let the shepherd leave the 99.
Let the old woman
light a lamp and sweep.
I will tell you only: *This will end.*

Rocks to Clouds

You cannot take these stones to school,
so you empty your pockets, your shoes,
your hands. Some mere pebbles
and other jagged rocks
threaded with something shiny
you want to call valuable.

Now that you have let go
of so much, your hair turns
to sand, your skin to sea spray.
The ocean wind blows you away.
Let go. Free yourself like the braided
strings that no longer hold kites
snaking down the empty beach.

A Box Made in Autumn

It matters how you fold things
like a napkin or your hands.

There are pin holes in the body
that light doesn't shine through.

It is raining. Don't use these words:
steam, smoke, fog. The color

of oranges has nothing to do
with their ripeness. Don't use

these words: *He is wheeled away.*
I walk to a room to wait. The phone

will ring, and I'll answer in a lost way. *Hello?*
Salt over the shoulder, four leaf clover.

I will catch the falling leaves on my tongue.

The Dusting

Every body wants. The tongue licks
that last hint of sugar from lips.

Fingers rub satin clean from the blanket's edge.
The soles of our feet sink into earth until the air

carries the odor of crushed grass.
Everyone wants more. The eyes

of the dying are wide open. The mouths
of the dying are wide open. The nostrils. The ears.

The hearts incessant: *More. More.*
Listen. A dark song folds the night clouds

into a clap of thunder. I will die.
There will be nothing

left but a wisp of smoke rising
from my open mouth like a Satin moth

wheeling towards the slow turning—
a kiss of white wing dust on my lips.

To the Man With His Back to the Chapel

I'm a silent rib, the curved derivative,
a harpist playing in the long hallway
to our bed. You make a bed out of leaves
and an exit of every door. Our skin
defines the borders between us.
Where are the tunnels and catacombs,
the dark paths to the underground city
for our emissaries or outlaws? So where
are the peacemakers with their bright flags
and easy-to-make rope bridges?
We're the footprint of a miracle,
the smoke of the just extinguished flame.
When it's over, let us stand forever
in this photo where there's no difference
between us and the near dusk.

The Sunken Narrative

Imagine a wooden schooner sailing
closely along a rugged coast.
Waves break along a ridge
of hidden reefs a mile offshore,
and the square-rigged canvas
flaps as a strong tidal current
sweeps the boat off its point
toward white-rimmed rocks.

Imagine years later someone writing:
*At the stern, a section of deck planking
remains, but the hull's broken
and the interior exposed. The fragile
wheel has long since disappeared,
the captain's quarters abandoned.*

Imagine someone logging artifacts
from the silt and mussel-covered wreck:
*a table set for four, a slim
wedding band, a broken mirror,
a cedar chest, and two gold coins.*

Imagine there were survivors
and that their story can be told,
how pieces of a broken mirror
can be collected and carefully
glued together again to make a circle.

My Daughter's Keepsake Rock

Listen to the stone—its story
of glacial rifts and tectonic shifts,
the many lessons of being broken,
cleft clean from a solid source
to free fall into the sea.
The story of the sloughing down
to smooth essential by surf and sand.
Learn how to go with the flow
then inhabit stillness on a beach.
A simple roundness, the mountain's center—
this weight in your open palm.

MALAIKA KING ALBRECHT's chapbook *Lessons in Forgetting* was published by Main Street Rag and was a finalist in the 2011 Next Generation Indie Book Awards and received honorable mention in the Brockman Campbell Award. Her second chapbook *Spill* was also published by Main Street Rag in 2011. Her poems have been published in many literary magazines and anthologies and nominated for the Pushcart Prize. Her poems have won awards in several contests, including at *Poetry Southeast*, the North Carolina Poetry Council, Salem College, and the Press 53 Open Awards. She's the founding editor of *Redheaded Stepchild*, an online magazine that accepts only poems that have been rejected elsewhere. She lives in Pinehurst, N.C. with her family and is a therapeutic riding instructor.

www.ingramcontent.com/pod-product-compliance
Lightning Source LLC
Chambersburg PA
CBHW022108040426
42451CB00007B/184